P9-DGL-524

Contents

Introduction

If you knew ways to make your life better, right now and for the future, would you try them?

We're guessing you would, and that's why we wrote this book. It's part of a series of eight books called the **Adding Assets Series for Kids.**

What Are Assets, Anyway?

When we use the word **assets**, we mean good things you need in your life and yourself.

We don't mean houses, cars, property, and jewelry—assets whose value is measured in money. We mean **Developmental Assets** that help you to be and become your best. Things like a close, loving family. A neighborhood where you feel safe. Adults you look up to and respect. And (sorry!) doing your homework.

There are 40 Developmental Assets in all. This book is about adding five of them to your life. They're called the **Social Competencies Assets.** "Competencies" is a big word for "skills" or "know-how." Social competencies help you make plans, choices, and friends. They help you get along with all kinds of people, even when you're different or you disagree. They help you resolve conflicts in a peaceful way so no one gets hurt. When you have social competencies, you feel comfortable around other people and good about yourself.

The Social Competencies Assets

Asset Name	What It Means
Planning and Decision Making	You think about the choices you make, and you're usually happy with your decisions. You know how to plan ahead.
Interpersonal Competence	You care about other people and their feelings. You enjoy making friends. When you feel angry or frustrated, you try to calm yourself down.
Cultural Competence	You know and are comfortable with people of different races, ethnic backgrounds, and cultures. You're also comfortable with your own cultural identity.
Resistance Skills	You stay away from people who could get you into trouble. You can say no to doing things that are dangerous or wrong.
Peaceful Conflict Resolution	You try to resolve conflicts in a peaceful way, without using harsh words or violent actions.

Other books in the series are about the other 35 assets.* That may seem like a lot, but don't worry. You don't have to add them all at once. You don't have to

* If you're curious to know what the other assets are, you can read the whole list on pages 80–81.

add them in any particular order. But the sooner you can add them to your life, the better.

Why You Need Assets

An organization called Search Institute surveyed hundreds of thousands of kids and teens across the United States. Their researchers found that some kids have a fairly easy time growing up, while others don't. Some kids get involved in harmful behaviors or dangerous activities, while others don't.

What makes the difference? Developmental Assets! Kids who have them are more likely to do well. Kids who don't have them are less likely to do well.

Maybe you're thinking, "Why should I have to add my own assets? I'm just a kid!" Because kids have the power to make choices in their lives. You can choose to sit back and wait for other people to help you, or you can choose to help yourself. You can also work with other people who care about you and want to help.

Many of the ideas in this book involve working with other people—like your parents, grandparents, aunts, uncles, and other family grown-ups. And your teachers, neighbors, coaches, Scout leaders, and religious leaders. They can all help add assets for you and with you.

It's likely that many of the adults in your life are already helping. In fact, an adult probably gave you this book to read.

How to Use This Book

Start by choosing **one** asset to add. Read the stories at the beginning and end of that chapter. The stories are examples of the assets in everyday life. Then pick **one** idea and try it. See how it goes After that, try another idea, or mo on to another asset.

Don't worry about being perfect or getting it right. Know that by trying, you're doing something great for yourself.

The more assets you add, the better you'll feel about yourself and your future. Soon you won't be a kid anymore. You'll be a teenager. Because you have assets, you'll feel and be a lot more sure of yourself. You'll make better decisions. You'll have a head start on success.

We wish you the very best as you add assets to your life.

Pamela Espeland and Elizabeth Verdick
Minneapolis, MN

A Few Words About Families

Kids today live in many different kinds of families.

Maybe you live with one or both of your parents. Maybe you live with other adult relatives—aunts and uncles, grandparents, grown-up brothers or sisters or cousins.

Maybe you live with a stepparent, foster parent, or guardian. Maybe you live with one of your parents and his or her life partner.

In this series, we use the word **parents** to describe the adults who care for you in your home. We also use **family adults**, **family grown-ups**, and **adults at home.** When you see any of these words, think of your own family, whatever kind it is.

Planning and Decision Making

What it means: You think about the choices you make, and you're usually happy with your decisions. You know how to plan ahead.

GRaHaM & LeoN'S StoRy

"This is so cool, doing our report together," says Graham.

"Yeah, ours is going to be the *best*," his friend Leon replies.

They bend their heads over their desks to start planning. Their report on bones is due Friday, which means they have four days to complete the work.

"How should we divide things up?" Graham asks.

"Easy. You draw the cover 'cause you're good at art. We'll both do our own paragraphs, like we're supposed to. Then I'll type it all up on my dad's computer and print it out."

After school, Graham tells his grandma about the bones project. She helps him find black construction paper and white paint. "I'll do the cover first," he says, painting a large skull. He leaves black spaces for eye sockets, nose holes, and a wide grin.

"Impressive," says his grandma.

"Wait until you see the lettering I'm doing for the title," Graham answers. He chooses a small paintbrush to spell out "BONES" in bone-shaped letters. When he's finished, he hangs it on the fridge with magnets to dry.

The next day at school, Graham tells Leon about the cover.

"Awesome!" says Leon.

"Did you work on your part?" Graham asks him.

"Not yet, but I'll get to it," Leon replies.

That evening, Graham reviews his worksheets about bones so he can write one of the paragraphs he's required to do. He carefully prints, "If people didn't have bones, they would fall to the floor like a puddle of skin and muscles." He adds facts and then checks the spelling of bone names like *patella,* which is the knee bone. "Tomorrow I'll work on the second paragraph," he tells himself.

Graham sticks to his plan and finishes the second paragraph the next night. He's proud of himself, but something's bothering him. Leon had admitted at recess that he still hadn't started his part of the project. "What if he doesn't get it done?" Graham worries. "What if he ruins everything?"

Graham has the *Planning and Decision Making* asset, but he's not sure his project partner does.

Think about your own life. Are you good at planning ahead? Do you think about the choices and decisions you make? Are you happy with most of your choices and decisions?

If **YES**, keep reading to learn ways to make this asset even stronger.

If **NO,** keep reading to learn ways to add this asset to your life.

You can also use these ideas to help add this asset

Facts!

Kids with the *Planning and Decision Making* asset:

✔ get better grades in school

✔ feel more independent

✔ are less likely to use cigarettes, alcohol, and other drugs

for other people—like your friends, family members, neighbors, and kids at school.

ways to Add This Asset

 **AT HOME**

Be a Planner. Some kids think, "*Planning*—that's for grown-ups." But the truth is you get further in life if you have an idea of where you're going and what you want to do. You can start small by simply thinking of your plans for today. What do you have to do at school? After school? During sports or your club? Make a to-do list. Check off items (including chores and homework) as you complete them. You'll feel a sense of satisfaction when you look at what you've checked off.

A message for you

To be a planner, get a planner. Maybe your school has a certain kind of planner you're supposed to use. If not, you can find day planners at any office supplies store. It's possible that someone at home has an extra planner you can use so you won't have to buy one. Ask a grown-up to help you learn how to use it. On school mornings, put your planner in your backpack, then remember to bring it home at the end of the day. That way, you'll always know what comes next and what you need to accomplish. This is a guaranteed way to get more organized, which helps you feel more in control of your time and your life.

Be a Goal Setter. Don't think "Goals, who needs them?" because *everyone* does. Goals give life meaning and purpose. Think of something you *really* want to do. Maybe you'd like to buy your own camera, score higher on your next math test, or finish a book you're reading. Maybe you're thinking further ahead—something like "I want to be a veterinarian." Guess what? You have a goal!

Set a Smart Goal. There are smart goals and not-so-smart goals. Smart goals are within your reach—maybe not today or tomorrow, but someday. They help you feel excited and inspired. To set a smart goal, make it (1) positive, (2) specific, and (3) realistic. ***Examples:*** "Study between 6:00 and 7:00 p.m. three evenings this week so I'm ready for my spelling test." "Save three-quarters of my allowance for six months to put toward the bike I want." Not-so-smart goals are unrealistic. They set you up for disappointment and make you feel like a failure. ***Example:*** "I want to wake up tomorrow and be a famous actor or rock star."

Write It Down. Planners and goal-setters have something in common: They write things down. Writing your plans and goals on paper (or on the computer to print out) gives you something to look at, touch, and strive for. Now that you've thought of a goal, it's time to put it into words. Write your goal in positive, specific language. You can start off with "I will . . ." or "I want to . . . ." Make sure it's something you *really* want to do—and something that's possible for you to do.

Plan Your Steps. If you've written down your goal and you're excited to get going, you're ready to plan the steps you need to take. This isn't always easy, so ask a family grown-up to help you. Any goal needs a timeline—you can't do it all in one day. For fun, you can draw footprints and write your steps in them. *Example:* MY GOAL: "I will organize my backpack and my desk at home so I'll feel more prepared at school."

Monday—Empty backpack, throw out old papers & trash.

Tuesday—Clean out pencil case & sharpen pencils.

Thursday—Clean off my desk.

Wednesday—Reorganize folders.

Friday—Get desk supplies (planner, markers, tape).

Saturday—Take a break!

Sunday—Put planner & homework in back-pack so I'm ready for Monday.

Practice Making Good Decisions. When you're faced with a decision, what do you do? The first thing that comes into your head? That's called a "snap decision." Or maybe you procrastinate and don't decide at all. The next time you have an important decision to make, try this instead: Get a piece of paper and divide it into two columns. Write "Pros" at the top of the left-hand column, "Cons" at the top of the right-hand column. Then list all the pros (good things) and cons (not-so-good things) about your decision. If the Pros list is longer or stronger, you're doing the right thing. If the Cons list is longer or stronger, re-think your decision.

> **Tip:** You won't always have time to think things through so carefully. When you have to make a quick decision, base it on your values—the guiding beliefs you've learned from your parents and other family adults, your faith community, and your role models.

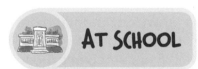 **At School**

★ Look around at the successful students in your school. Chances are, they know how to plan ahead. Do they use student planners or to-do lists? Do they turn in their homework on time? Are they usually prepared for classes and tests? See what you can learn from them.

★ Don't let long-term projects get the best of you. Divide and conquer! Break a big, scary project into small, doable steps. Write them down. Check them off as you complete them.

> **TiP:** Need help figuring out the steps? Ask a teacher. Almost any teacher would rather help kids plan for long-term projects than hear excuses about why they will be late.

 ## IN YOUR NEIGHBORHOOD

★ Volunteer to help plan a neighborhood event. Can you go door-to-door with a grown-up and hand out flyers about a block party? Can you organize a day of games for little kids? What about a neighborhood clean-up day?

★ Talk with neighbors you look up to and admire. Ask them about their goals in life. What were their goals when they were your age? What was the first big goal they can remember reaching? How have goals helped them get where they are today? Do they have any tips they can share with you?

IN YOUR FAITH COMMUNITY

★ Talk with your religion class or youth group about how your values affect your decisions. Have you ever made a decision that went against your values? How did you feel about that?

WITH YOUR FRIENDS

★ When friends have important decisions to make, they usually talk to each other. They get each other's opinions before deciding what to do. Make a pact with your friends to help each other make good decisions.

★ Plan a surprise party for another friend. This could be a birthday party, a congratulations party, or a just-because-we-like-you party.

Start Adding!

Pick at least ONE idea you've read here and give it a try. Then think about or write about what happened. Will you try other ways to make better decisions and plan ahead?

Back to Graham & Leon's Story

By Thursday, Graham is more than worried—he's freaking out. Leon hasn't done one thing for their project, and they have to turn it in tomorrow.

At lunch, Graham sits near Jenna, his best friend from another classroom. He tells her about the project and Leon's failure to start working on it. "Some partner, huh?" he says with a scowl.

"It's a problem," she agrees. "What are you going to do about it?"

"I have no clue. My grandma says I should tell the teacher. But I don't want to get Leon in trouble. I guess I could just do all the work myself and put both our names on the report. But that's so unfair!"

"That's what I'd do," says Jenna. "I wouldn't let my grade go down because I got stuck with someone who doesn't do the work."

"I don't know . . ." Graham replies.

"Well, you'd better do something soon," Jenna says.

Graham thinks about his problem all through recess. By the time everyone heads back indoors, he's made his decision.

He finds Leon at his desk and says, "Leon, we really have to get the project done. Can I come to your house after school so we can work together on the paragraphs? Would your dad let us use his computer?"

Leon looks at him and says, "Yeah, *definitely*. I'm glad you had this idea because I'm not getting anywhere on the project." Then he asks hesitantly, "Are you mad at me?"

Graham replies, "Let's just get it done and it'll all be fine, okay?"

"Okay, come by at four o'clock. I promise I'll be ready to work!"

Graham smiles at his friend and sits down at his desk. He feels relieved that he made a good choice and handled the situation on his own.

Interpersonal Competence

What it means: You care about other people and their feelings. You enjoy making friends. When you feel angry or frustrated, you try to calm yourself down.

Maria, Jordy, & Bel's Story

"Hi, guys!" Maria waves to Jordy and Belinda, her two closest friends. It's Friday evening at the YMCA, and the three of them are ready for their usual night of fun in the pool.

"We'll race you, Jordy," challenges Belinda. "If we're out of the locker room and into the pool first, we get dibs on which game to start with."

Maria and Belinda like diving to the bottom of the pool to grab the weighted rubber hoops, but Jordy's favorite game is Marco Polo.

"All right, I'm out of here!" cries Jordy, racing past them toward the men's locker room.

The girls rush to change into their bathing suits and head for the pool. Jordy is already treading water when they get there. "Ha!" he says, laughing. "I pick Marco Polo."

"No fair!" says Belinda, a little too loudly. Some of the other swimmers turn to look at her. "I slipped on that puddle over there, and Miss Slowpoke took her sweet time getting her suit on."

Maria feels a little hurt, but she says in a calm voice, "Jordy got here first, Bel, and it's no big deal to play our game second."

"Yeah, but I'm sick of Marco Polo," Belinda answers. "And besides, Jordy always cheats."

"I do not!" he protests.

"Do so!" Belinda yells. Her face reddens and her eyes squint, sure signs that a screaming fit could happen at any moment.

Jordy and Maria look at each other, knowing that Belinda will probably keep arguing until she gets her way. In silent agreement, they both decide to give in.

"Okay, have it your way, Bel," Jordy says quietly.

"I'll get the hoops," Maria adds, paddling to the area where the pool toys are stored.

Belinda beams. "This will be way more fun anyway!" she says. Then she shouts, "Look out for Shark Girl!" She dives deep and grabs her friends' legs.

They can't help but laugh when she reaches down and starts tickling their feet.

Maria and Jordy have the *Interpersonal Competence* asset, but Belinda doesn't.

Think about your own life. Do you notice how other people feel? Does it matter to you if they're happy or sad, angry or upset? Is making friends easy or hard for you? Do you know how to calm yourself down instead of losing your temper?

If **YES,** keep reading to learn ways to make this asset even stronger.

If **NO,** keep reading to learn ways to add this asset to your life.

> ## Facts!
>
> **Kids with the *Interpersonal Competence* asset:**
>
> ✓ have fewer behavior problems
>
> ✓ do better in school
>
> ✓ have higher self-esteem

You can also use these ideas to help add this asset for other people—like your friends, family members, neighbors, and kids at school.

ways to Add This Asset

 AT HOME

Learn More About Your Feelings. Every day, you probably experience a range of emotions—everything from happiness to sadness to anger. At times, you may be worried and stressed, or you might feel like you're bouncing off the walls with energy. Feelings can be hard to understand.

So, how do you start getting to know your feelings better? One way is to keep a Feelings Journal. Get any kind of notebook or a diary with a lock. Date each entry and spend time writing about things that happened at school or at home, how you felt, and how you reacted. Writing can help you express your emotions and realize that it's okay to have strong feelings.

> **TiP:** Journals are private, so store yours in a place where no one will look. It's easier to be honest in your writing when you don't have to worry about someone peeking. But know that you can share what you've written with a caring adult, if you want to.

Talk to Your Family. Is there a family grown-up you trust enough to talk with about your deepest emotions? Maybe you confide in your dad or mom, an older sibling, an aunt or uncle, or a grandparent. Find at least one person to go to—someone you can count on to listen.

Build a Feelings Vocabulary. Do you have the words you need to describe your feelings? Do you know what other people mean when they talk about their feelings? A feelings vocabulary can help you say what you mean and understand feelings better—yours and other people's. Look up words about feelings in a dictionary. Use a thesaurus to find synonyms (different words for the same or similar feeling). Listen to other people talk about their feelings. Ask for help explaining your feelings.

20 Cool Words for Your Feelings Vocabulary

If you don't know what a word means, look it up. Then think of a time when you might have felt that way. Practice using the word in a sentence. **Examples:** "I felt *ecstatic* when my mom said I could get a puppy." "I felt *mortified* when I bent over to pick up my backpack and split my pants!"

1. antsy
2. anxious
3. confident
4. depressed
5. ecstatic
6. enraged
7. enthusiastic
8. exhausted
9. fidgety
10. flabbergasted
11. furious
12. gloomy
13. horrified
14. mortified
15. puzzled
16. relaxed
17. self-conscious
18. serene
19. terrified
20. timid

Use Your Feelings Vocabulary. Instead of yelling, "Everyone just leave me alone!" you could say, "I'm mad right now because I forgot to bring home my library book, and my social studies project is due tomorrow. Now I won't be able to finish, and I'm worried I'll get a bad grade. I'm frustrated because school is closed, and there's no way to go back and get my book. And I'm about to lose it because I don't know what to do!" See the difference? Saying *how* you feel and *why* helps open the door to solving your problem. A caring adult at home can then offer some guidance or advice.

Know How to Calm Yourself Down. Did you know that calming yourself down is a skill? It takes practice. (There are plenty of grown-ups who don't have this skill yet. Have you ever seen a pro athlete go nuts and start yelling at the ref when a bad call is made? Have you heard about celebrities who throw public tantrums?) *Everyone* gets frustrated and angry, but a strong person can handle those feelings in a healthy way. Instead of shouting, hitting, or throwing a fit, you can tell yourself to *calm down*. Take a few slow, deep breaths. You can count to five in your head as you breathe in; count backwards from five as you breathe out. You'll feel calmer and more ready to deal with whatever has upset you. Practice this technique at home until you feel comfortable with it.

6 Things to Tell Yourself When You Need to Chill

1. "I can handle this."

2. "I'm going to be okay."

3. "I will let this roll off my back."

4. "I'm in control of my feelings."

5. "I'm strong enough to deal with this problem."

6. "I can find someone to help me."

Be Aware of Your Family's Feelings, Too. What do you usually do when someone at home seems sad, mad, or worried? Do you tiptoe away so you don't have to get involved? Do you wait until it blows over? Or do you ask what's up? Sometimes, it may be helpful for you to let the people in your family know you care and are willing to listen. ***Examples:*** You could tell a younger sibling, "I'm always here if you have a problem you want to talk about." You could say to your big brother, "You help me a lot, so let me know if I can help you." You could give a family adult a hug, a shoulder rub, or a handmade card that says "I love you."

AT SCHOOL

★ Make a new friend at school today. Is there someone you'd like to get to know? Think about something you could say to the person. ***Examples:*** "I've seen you skateboard around the park," or "You're new—where are you from?" or "Cool T-shirt. That's my favorite team." Then go up to the person in the hall, in the lunchroom, or at recess. Say hi, smile, and introduce yourself. Try starting a conversation. See if you have something in common. Most of all, be friendly and just be yourself.

★ The next time you get angry or frustrated at school—in class, at recess, in the lunch line, or wherever—calm yourself down. Use the technique described on pages 25–26. If your friends notice and ask what's up, offer to teach them the technique.

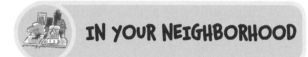

IN YOUR NEIGHBORHOOD

★ Your friends don't all have to be your age. In fact, the older you get, the more friends you'll have who are different ages, until age will hardly even matter. (Ask your parents or an older cousin about this.) Your own neighborhood might be the perfect place to make friends who are younger and older than you. Reach out to little kids. Spend time with older adults your parents know and like. Especially if your own grandparents are far away, you might really enjoy having a "grandma" or "grandpa" who lives across the street or down the hall.

IN YOUR FAITH COMMUNITY

★ When teens were asked what kinds of things they'd like to learn more about from their faith community, the top answer was "how to make friends and be a friend." How does your faith community help kids do this? Are there clubs for kids? Activities? Camp-outs? If there are, get involved. Your faith community is a great place to make friends who share your values.

 WITH YOUR FRIENDS

★ Play Feelings Charades. One person acts out a feeling (using body language and facial expressions, but no words) and everyone else tries to name the feeling. *Examples:* snooty, silly, embarrassed, lovestruck, bossy.

> **TiP:** Leave room for close-enoughs. If someone acts out "angry" and people guess "mad," that's close enough. If someone acts out "sad" and people guess "bummed out" or "down in the dumps," that's close enough.

★ As a group, agree that it's okay to talk about and show your feelings. (This is often easier for girls than for boys, but boys have feelings, too.) Try to be more aware of each other's feelings. If someone seems sad or worried, don't just ignore it. Say, "Are you okay?" Or, "You seem kind of sad today. Want to talk about it?"

A special message for boys

Boys often believe they need to be tough and keep their feelings to themselves. They may think that showing feelings is a sign of weakness, and talking about feelings . . . forget it! That's for wimps! So they stuff their feelings inside and pretend they don't even exist. Because of this, many boys feel sad, confused, lonely, and scared. These feelings can become so strong that some boys end up hurting other people or themselves. Don't let this happen to you. Find someone to talk to—a friend who understands, a family adult who will listen, a teacher or coach or school counselor who will never make fun of you. Your feelings are part of who you are. You have the right to express them.

Start Adding!

Pick at least ONE idea you've read here and give it a try. Then think about or write about what happened. Will you try another way to tune into other people's feelings? To make a new friend? To calm yourself when you're upset?

Back to Maria, Jordy, & Bel's Story

After swimming, the friends agree to get changed and head for the recreation room. They find an open Ping-Pong table and Bel says, "I'll round up another player so we can play doubles."

Maria and Jordy hit the ball back and forth as they wait. After several minutes have passed, they wonder aloud why Bel hasn't yet returned.

"Maybe no one wants to play," Maria says.

"Don't worry," Jordy says. "If no one wants to, Bel will *make* them want to."

Maria snorts, "Yeah, she'll twist their arm—I mean for real!"

"She'll bust some heads," Jordy says with a laugh.

"Can we help it if our friend thinks she's the boss of the world?" Maria asks.

"And has worse temper tantrums than my little brother?" Jordy replies.

Maria giggles as Jordy mimics Belinda's angry expression.

THWACK!

Maria and Jordy both jump at the sound of Bel's Ping-Pong paddle slapping the table.

"How much did you hear?" Jordy asks Belinda softly.

Tears spring into her eyes. "All of it," she says. She turns and runs out of the room.

Unsure what to do next, Maria and Jordy lean against the Ping-Pong table, staring at the ground.

"We should apologize to her," Jordy announces.

"Yeah, we should, right away. Do you think she'll forgive us?"

"I hope so. I feel really bad for talking about her that way," says Jordy.

"Me, too. Come on, let's go find her." Maria pulls his arm.

Just as they open the rec room doors, Belinda bounds back in, her face a tear-stained mess.

"I'm sorry!" the three friends say in unison. Then, "Jinx!" they all say at once and start laughing.

"Now what?" Maria asks.

"Uh . . . Ping-Pong?" Jordy suggests.

Maria and Jordy look at Bel hopefully. "Sure," she agrees. "But one thing first." After a pause, she says, "I know I can be a pain sometimes. I'm sorry. I'll work on it, okay?"

Her friends smile at her. "Come on," they say, putting their arms around her and leading her to the Ping-Pong table.

"I get first serve—or else!" Bel warns, grabbing her paddle. "*Kidding!* I'm only kidding," she adds with a grin.

Cultural Competence

What it means: You know and are comfortable with people of different races, ethnic backgrounds, and cultures. You're also comfortable with your own cultural identity.

Diego's Story

"Mom?" Diego asks while riding home from chess club. "Sometimes I don't know who to play with during recess. I feel stupid hanging around by myself."

"Hmmm," replies his mom, looking at him in the rearview mirror. "It's hard being new. I still feel a little lost here myself. Have you asked to join in when the kids are playing kickball and stuff like that?"

Diego sighs and looks out the window. "Nah, everyone's already got friends. It's not like home. No one really seems to notice me here."

"How about just going up and saying, 'My name's Diego, can I hang out with you?'" his mom suggests.

"It's not that easy. They might think I'm too different. When the teacher first introduced me to the class, someone said 'Diego—like the *cartoon* character!'"

"So?" his mom says, pulling into the parking lot of their apartment building.

"So I said, 'No, like Diego Rivera, the artist.' No one knew who I meant. Now some of the kids are calling me 'The Artist,' and not in a good way.

His mom turns to look at him in the backseat. "Hey, buddy," she says kindly. "Let's give the kids another chance to get to know you. We can have a few of them over for dinner, with some of our favorite foods. I'll make my famous salsa, and you and Dad can be in charge of the empanadas. Are you interested?"

Diego thinks it over for a few moments. Then he smiles into his mom's warm brown eyes. "I'm interested. I just hope some of the other kids will be!"

Diego is proud of who he is, and he has the *Cultural Competence* asset. Still, he's not always confident that others will like him.

Think about your own life. Do you know and hang out with people of different races, ethnic backgrounds, and cultural backgrounds? Are you proud of who you are and where you come from?

If **YES,** keep reading to learn ways to make this asset even stronger.

If **NO,** keep reading to learn ways to add this asset to your life.

You can also use these ideas to help add this asset for other people—like your friends, family members, neighbors, and kids at school.

> ## Facts!
>
> **Kids with the *Cultural Competence* asset:**
>
> ✓ are more accepting of people of different races and culture
>
> ✓ are less likely to *stereotype* others (to judge them or assume things about them without really knowing them)
>
> ✓ have stronger leadership skills

ways to Add This Asset

 **AT HOME**

Explore Your Own Cultural History. Talk to the adults at home about your cultural roots. Where do you come from? Who were your ancestors? If you can't track down this information, ask your family grown-ups and other relatives to tell you about their cultural heritage. Learn more about your own racial or ethnic group by checking out books at the library or surfing the Internet (ask an adult first). If you're lucky enough to have museums or cultural centers where you live, visit them with your family. Talk about what you see and learn.

Try New Foods. Maybe you're used to eating peanut butter and jelly sandwiches or macaroni and cheese for nearly every meal. Lots of kids are! But there's a world of different foods out there just waiting for you. Talk to your mom or dad about trying some ethnic dishes or fruits and vegetables from other regions. Search together to find recipes that you're excited about (you can look in cookbooks or online). Have fun shopping for unusual ingredients and exploring flavors and spices. If you're not into cooking, how about going to an ethnic restaurant instead?

Experience New Things. Many communities observe ethnic holidays with special events or festivals. Often, these are listed in the local newspaper or posted on bulletin boards in park buildings. Keep an eye out for things that sound interesting, then see if your family would like to go. *Examples:* May 5 is Cinco de Mayo, a day that honors Latino culture. Juneteenth—June 19th—is a day to celebrate the end of slavery in the United States. (Some communities celebrate Juneteenth for a week or even a month.) For many cultures (Chinese, Korean, and Vietnamese, to name a few), the New Year starts on a different day than January 1. Native American tribes hold pow-wows throughout the year, and the public is often welcome.

Shine a Light on Your Stereotypes. When we *stereotype* other people, we judge them or assume things about them without really knowing them. Try this exercise. In your journal (so it's private), write "Jocks always . . . ,"  then write *the very first thing that comes into your mind.* Don't think about it; just write it. Do the same for the sentence starters in the box on page 41. Afterward, look at what you wrote. These are some of your stereotypes. Guess what? Everyone has stereotypes. The way to fight back against stereotypes, racism, and other wrong ideas about people isn't to pretend they don't exist. It's to admit they exist, then work to change your own thoughts, attitudes, and actions. It won't be easy, but you can do it—and you'll be setting a good example for others.

TiP: Start by getting to know some people you usually stereotype. Once you learn more about them and maybe make friends with them, your stereotypes will fade away. **TiP Too:** Talk with your parents or other family grown-ups about stereotypes. Ask what stereotypes they have—or used to have.

What Are Your Stereotypes?

Don't think about what to write. Don't worry about writing the "right" thing. Just finish each sentence with the first thing that comes into your mind.

* Girls always . . .

* Smart kids always . . .

* Black people always . . .

* Boys always . . .

* Asian people always . . .

* Old people always . . .

* Hispanic people always . . .

* Little kids always . . .

* Poor people always . . .

* White people always . . .

* People with disabilities always . . .

* Rich people always . . .

* People with tattoos always . . .

* Teenagers always . . .

 **AT SCHOOL**

Don't Put Up with Racism. Maybe your friends or the kids in your neighborhood tease others who are different. And maybe this leads to fights or hurt feelings. You don't have to be a part of this—and you don't have to stay quiet when it happens. Speaking out against racism takes courage, whether you're the one being teased or not. To tell people you don't like that kind of taunting, you could say, "That joke isn't funny, it's hurtful," or "I don't like that kind of talk, and I'm leaving right now." Don't laugh at cruel jokes or ignore them. Set a good example by treating all people with respect.

Mix It Up. What's it like at your school? Do the African-American kids mostly hang out with each other? What about the white kids? The Hispanic kids? The Asian kids? What about you and your friends? Make a change. Invite kids from other races, ethnic backgrounds, or culture to join your game at recess. Sit at a different table for lunch.

Get a Pen Pal or Email Pal from Another Country. See if your teacher will let you do this as a school project. It might be something the whole class can do.

TiP: Check with a parent or teacher before registering for anything online.

Places to Find Pen Pals or Email Pals

Circle of Friends PenPal Club
members.agirlsworld.com
For girls only. Write to other girls ages 7–17 around the world; create your own online page; make a buddy list (and write to lots of friends at once). You must have a parent's permission to join, and there is an annual membership fee.

Kids' Space Connection
www.ks-connection.org
A free international meeting place for children and teachers. Use the Kids Connect Penpal Box to find pen pals from all over the world. Use the KS Messaging Center as your safe tool for communication. If you're under 13, you'll need to register with your parent or caregiver.

World Pen Pals
www.world-pen-pals.com
For a small fee, you'll receive a name and address, simple mailing directions, and a page of helpful hints. (Tell your teacher that classrooms get group rates.) If you're under 13, you'll need permission from a parent.

IN YOUR NEIGHBORHOOD

Broaden Your Horizons. Your local library is full of books about cultural history. You can find books that describe how kids in other countries live, or read stories and legends from different parts of the world. You can look at atlases and maps, or you can study the flags of other nations or find pictures of their money, stamps, or famous heroes. When you learn about other cultures, your mind expands, and so does your respect for people of different races and backgrounds.

Reach Out to Others. Get to know a larger variety of neighbors or members of your faith community. Make friends with kids who aren't the same age, race, gender (boy or girl), or religion as you. If some of them speak a different language, ask them to teach you some words and phrases. In turn, you can introduce them to your family's traditions.

IN YOUR FAITH COMMUNITY

★ Have you ever heard of a "sister" church, synagogue, or mosque? This is when two congregations form a special relationship. They communicate with each other, visit each other, and help each other. Often, "sisters" share the same faith but are located in different countries. Does your faith community have a "sister"? If it does, are the children and teens in touch with each other? Maybe you can help start an email exchange.

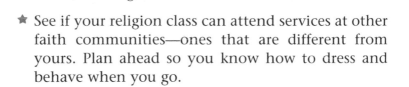

★ See if your religion class can attend services at other faith communities—ones that are different from yours. Plan ahead so you know how to dress and behave when you go.

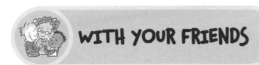

WITH YOUR FRIENDS

★ Look around at your circle of friends. Are you all pretty much the same? It's natural to want to be with people who share your likes and dislikes and maybe come from similar backgrounds. That's easy and comfortable to do. But it can make your world awfully small. Talk as a group about how to widen your circle and include other people. If your other friends don't want to do this, make some new friends on your own.

Start Adding!

Pick at least ONE idea you've read here and give it a try. Then think about or write about what happened. Will you try another idea to broaden your world and build your cultural competence?

Back to
Diego's
Story

Diego decides to ask some of the kids from chess club to come over for dinner. He invites Will, Maya, Antoine, and Dantrelle.

"Whoa!" exclaims Antoine as Diego opens the door to the apartment. "We could smell something delicious all the way out here in the hallway."

Maya and Dantrelle smile and say hi as they walk in. "Cool place," says Dantrelle.

"Thanks," Diego replies. He feels shy but happy that they've come. The night before, he'd been worried that no one would show up. "Will's already here," he tells the others. "He's in the kitchen with my parents, mashing up avocados for the guacamole."

Diego leads the way, then makes introductions. Will holds up his hands, which are covered in green goop, and wiggles them at everyone. "Guacamole is fun to make!" he says.

"Looks like you're making a mess," Maya laughs.

"Just wait, we're about to get messier," says Diego's dad with a smile. He wipes down the kitchen table and asks everyone to wash their hands and gather around to make empanadas. Then he pours a mound of flour in the middle of the table and explains how they're going to make special dough using an old recipe of Diego's great-grandmother's. "I'll mix the dough, then you guys will each get to knead it. Sound good?"

Diego watches as his friends take turns, and he listens while they talk about chess club and school. Soon their hands are covered with flour and bits of sticky dough. Diego relaxes and starts telling everyone about himself, his family, and their move from New Mexico.

Next, Diego's dad pushes the dough into a log shape and breaks off pieces for everyone. He brings out a mixture of cooked meat, olives, and hard-boiled eggs, which he'd put together the night before. "You're going to flatten your dough pieces, put a scoop of the mixture in, and then wrap it up, like this," he explains, demonstrating each step.

"Oh! They're kind of like dumplings," Maya says.

Before long, the empanadas go into the oven, and the wonderful scent of pastry and spicy meat fills the air. Diego's mom tells the kids to sit in the family room, and she puts hot nachos, homemade salsa, and guacamole on the coffee table. Then she pours lemonade for everyone and returns to the kitchen.

"This is so much fun, Diego!" exclaims Dantrelle. "Why haven't you invited us over sooner?"

"Yeah," adds Antoine. "I always thought you were really good at chess, but you seemed so quiet, like you were shy or didn't like us."

"I liked you!" Diego says quickly, "but I thought you didn't like *me!*"

"Well, whatever! Just pass the chips, okay?" Maya says, laughing.

Diego smiles and looks around. He realizes that, for the first time, his family's new apartment is starting to feel like home.

"So," says Will, "can we come over for dinner tomorrow night, too?"

Resistance Skills

What it means: You stay away from people who could get you into trouble. You can say no to doing things that are dangerous or wrong.

Maddie & Krista's Story

Maddie can't wait for Alexia's slumber party. Alexia is the coolest girl in fifth grade, with a group of loyal friends who follow her every move. The slumber part is for her birthday. Maddie knows that Alexia lives in a huge house, and that all the girls will get to sleep in the basement, where there's a big-screen TV.

Actually, Maddie isn't sure why she and her best friend, Krista, were even invited. Alexia usually ignores both of them, but for some reason, she's decided to be nice for a change.

On the night of the party, Maddie's mom picks Krista up and drives both girls to Alexia's. "I'll bet she'll really like the present you girls got her," says Maddie's mom. Maddie thinks about how she and Krista went in on the gift together and added some of their own allowance money to pay for it. They wanted to give Alexia the best computer game they could find.

The party is a total blast, and everyone stuffs themselves on pizza, ice cream, and cake. Then Alexia yells, "Dance party!" All the girls run down to the basement and turn the music on. Maddie and Krista join the dancers, and Maddie pretends not to notice when some of Alexia's friends point at Krista behind her back and imitate—badly—some of her moves.

Later, Alexia opens her presents. She hugs each friend afterward—all except Krista and Maddie. But she thanks them politely, and Maddie feels hopeful that Alexia will accept the two of them into her group.

As night falls, the girls tell ghost stories and fortunes. Alexia stands up and announces, "I predict that we will play Truth or Dare."

Krista catches Maddie's eye, looking worried. They get into a circle, and each girl at the party takes a turn choosing "Truth" or "Dare." At first, everyone picks "Truth." Alexia gets an exaggerated look of disappointment on her face. "Come on, you guys! This is a party—isn't anyone going to take a dare?" She looks pointedly at Maddie.

"Maddie," she says, "*you* seem like you want to be cool—how about doing a dare?"

Maddie feels confused, and something's telling her that Alexia has a plan. But another part of her desperately wants to fit in.

Before Maddie can say a word, Krista pipes up with, "Dare. I'll do a dare."

Everyone turns to her in surprise. Alexia smiles.

Maddie's and Krista's *Resistance Skills* are about to be tested.

Think about your own life. Do you usually avoid troublemakers? Do you have the strength to say no when friends and others ask you to do things that might be wrong or dangerous? Can you stand your ground?

If **YES**, keep reading to learn ways to make this asset even stronger.

If **NO**, keep reading to learn ways to add this asset to your life.

Facts!

Kids with the *Resistance Skills* asset:

✔ have fewer behavior problems

✔ are less likely to use alcohol and other drugs

✔ get along better with others

You can also use these ideas to help add this asset for other people—like your friends, family members, neighbors, and kids at school.

ways to Add This Asset

 **At Home**

Respect Yourself. Self-respect is a basic: You've got to have it if you want to be strong in this world. Do you respect yourself? Do you feel good about yourself and have confidence in who you are? No matter what anyone says, you're a unique individual with original thoughts and creative ideas. No one else on earth is exactly like you. Write down five cool things about you (no one has to see this list). *Examples:* "I am loyal to my friends." "I like collecting rocks." "I take care of my body." "I have a family who loves me." "I draw funny comic strips." If you can come up with more than five, go for it. Look at your list whenever you need a reminder that you're important and one-of-a-kind. Add to it often.

A message for you

You've been reading about **assets**—good things all kids need in their lives to grow up strong and healthy. Even if you're adding assets to your life every day, there will be times when you're tested (and we don't mean like the tests you take at school). People will pressure you to take risks that aren't right for you. Other kids will push you to do dares, lie, cheat, steal, smoke cigarettes, take drugs, or do lots of other things that could hurt you now and in the future. Those kids may claim that these things are "cool" or show that you're "tough" or "grown-up." When you have **resistance skills**, you're strong enough to say no to these pressures. You have the self-respect to stay on your own path.

Talk to Your Parents. Ask them about a time when they were pressured to do something risky or dangerous. What did they do? Maybe they said no. Or maybe they gave in and got into trouble or worse. What did they learn from this experience?

> **TiP:** This is a great opportunity to talk to your parents about something you're being pressured to do. Ask for help saying no.

List Your Adult Helpers. Who do you count on for help and support? Your parents? Other family members? Teachers? Religious leaders? Neighbors you know well? Your friends' parents? These are the grown-ups you can go to when the going gets tough. Write their names on a list and keep it in your wallet, purse, or backpack. It will remind you that there are people who care about you. If your list includes people outside your family, ask them the best way to contact them. In person? By phone? By email, instant messaging, or text messaging? When you're having problems or being pressured, reach out to a grown-up on your list.

Be True to Yourself. If someone says, "Come on—everyone is doing it!" that's your cue to tell yourself, "I'm not everyone. I'm me!" Besides, "everyone" is not doing whatever the person is trying to get you to do. Look around and see for yourself.

Know How to Say No. Ask a family member to help you role-play resisting peer pressure and saying no. (See the list of role plays on pages 60–61.) This way, you'll be more prepared if you're pressured by someone at school or in your neighborhood. Practice using confident body language. Stand tall, look the person in the eye, and speak in a firm voice. Try different ways of staying no. Last but not least, practice your exit. Learn how to walk away with your head high, even if the person teases you. You could also practice running to find an adult helper.

> **TiP:** Saying no may be hard the first time, but it gets easier. It's kind of like weight training. The more reps you do, the stronger you become!

9 Ways to Say No

1. "I don't want to do that."
2. "Count me out."
3. "I'm not interested."
4. "Thanks, but no thanks."
5. "Forget it."
6. "No way."
7. "That's not for me."
8. "No—and I'm not going to change my mind."
9. "I'm out of here!"

For fun, you can say no in languages other than English. *Examples:*

Arabic: *la*	Mandarin Chinese: *bu dui*
French: *non*	Navajo: *ndaga'*
German: *nein*	Russian: *nyet*
Hebrew: *lo*	Somali: *maya*
Hmong: *tsis*	Urdu: *nahin*
Icelandic: *nei*	Vietnamese: *không*
Japanese: *iie*	Wolof: *deedeet*
Korean: *animnida*	Zulu: *cha*

You probably have friends who speak more than one language. Ask them to share some cool ways to say no.

AT SCHOOL

★ Sometimes kids pressure other kids *not* to succeed in school. They call them "teacher's pet" (or worse) if they care about school and try to do well. Think about what's best for you and your future. Do you really want to do poorly in school just to fit in? That won't help you form the study habits you need to get through high school and college (if you decide to go to college someday). Find other kids who take school seriously. Hang out with them and listen to them.

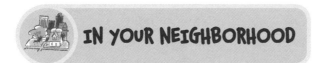

IN YOUR NEIGHBORHOOD

★ Almost every neighborhood has troublemakers. You probably know who they are in your neighborhood. Maybe they're older kids who make fun of or bully younger kids. Maybe they throw trash in your neighbors' yards or spray graffiti on signs or buildings. Maybe they try to get younger kids, including you, to follow along. They may pretend to be your friends, but what they really want is to have power over you. If you're being hassled, tell your mom, dad, or another family adult. Talk about ways to avoid troublemakers and stay out of their way.

★ To the younger kids in your neighborhood, *you're* the older kid. Remember this and try to be a good example— someone they can look up to.

 IN YOUR FAITH COMMUNITY

★ Talk with your religion class or youth group about building resistance skills. How can your faith help you say no to doing things that are dangerous or wrong? How can your values help you resist negative peer pressure?

★ As a group, role-play different situations and ways to respond. See pages 60–61 for ideas. Also see "9 Ways to Say No" on page 57.

12 Role Plays to Try

1. Someone wants you to dress or act in a way that doesn't feel right to you.

2. Someone wants you to be their girlfriend or boyfriend, but you just want to be friends.

3. A kid you look up to tries to get you to smoke a cigarette.

2. You like a certain kind of music, but your friends think it's stupid.

5. Someone wants you to sneak out after dark.

6. Other kids make fun of you for doing well in school.

7. Friends are trying to get you to drop out of scouts, but you like scouts.

8. Some of your friends have started bullying a younger kid, and they want you to join in.

9. One of your friends isn't doing so well in math. He wants you to help him cheat on the next big test.

10. A friend has started shoplifting. She says it's really exciting, and she wants you to go along with her next time.

11. You're at a party where kids start telling racist jokes. You don't think they're funny, but everyone else seems to.

12. You're the only one of your friends who wears a helmet when you ride your board or bike. The other kids have started calling you a dork.

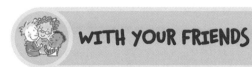

WITH YOUR FRIENDS

★ Make a pact with your best and closest friends. Agree to be each other's safety net and back each other up when the pressure is on. Help each other make safe, smart choices. Promise that you'll never push each other into doing stuff that's wrong or dangerous. These are promises that true friends make—and keep. If you want, you can put your pact in writing and have everyone sign it.

Start Adding!

Pick at least ONE idea you've read here and give it a try. Then think about or write about what happened. Will you try another way to avoid troublemakers and build your resistance skills?

Back to
**Maddie &
Krista's
Story**

Alexia slides over to Krista and says, "I knew one of you would do a dare."

Maddie sees the expression on Krista's face—a mix of pride and fear—and Maddie wants to protect her. "I'll do it with her," she says quickly, surprising herself.

Alexia grins. "Even better." She goes to a drawer and pulls out a large pair of pruning shears, the kind Maddie's dad uses for gardening.

"Oh, right," Maddie thinks. "She just happened to have those handy!" Then she turns to Krista and whispers, "This is a set-up."

"Just wait," Krista replies, watching Alexia closely.

"Here's your dare," says Alexia, holding up the shears. She walks to the sliding glass door, and everyone follows. She points to the neighbor's backyard, just visible in the moonlight. "Aren't those roses pretty?" she asks. "I dare you to cut enough of them to fill that vase." She points to an enormous vase on a nearby table.

Krista reaches her hand out for the shears, and Alexia slides the door open. Everyone watches as Maddie and Krista walk barefoot through the grass.

As Maddie approaches the garden, she sees that the bushes are covered in red, pink, and white blooms. "Someone planted all these," she thinks. "Whoever it is takes good care of them, too."

Krista reaches toward one of the bushes to cut the blooms, but Maddie quietly says, "Don't."

"But if we do, we'll be cool, like Alexia said," Krista answers.

"Do you really care what she thinks?"

Krista takes a while to answer. "No," she laughs. "Actually, I *don't*. What am I doing holding these giant scissors in the dark, about to bring a bunch of roses to someone I hardly even like?"

Maddie smiles, thinking how glad she is to have Krista as her best friend.

"What do we do now?" Krista asks.

"I say we go back in there, pack up our stuff, and call one of our parents to come get us."

"Good idea," Krista replies.

And so they do.

Peaceful Conflict Resolution

What it means: You try to resolve conflicts in a peaceful way, without using harsh words or violent actions.

Keisha's Story

Keisha punts the football with all her might and watches it soar toward her older brothers.

"Got it!" yells Billy.

"No, it's mine!" shouts Jerome, sprinting toward the ball. He leaps and catches it in the tips of his fingers. "Nice one, Keish—"

Before he can finish, Jerome tackles him hard and they both go tumbling across the grass. The two of them wrestle for the ball as Keisha runs toward them.

"How'd you like *that* kick, guys? You taught me everything I know . . . ." She stops short when she realizes that her brothers aren't playing around—they're really fighting.

"Come on, Billy, Jerome! Stop it!" she yells, afraid they might hurt each other.

The boys ignore her. "Let go!" Jerome yells. "No, *you* let go!" Billy yells back.

"Fine!" says Keisha. "I'm getting Dad." She stalks off while her brothers grunt and roll around on the ground behind her. At the last minute, she returns to them and aims a swift kick at her brothers' legs. Then she runs toward the house.

"Ow!" one of them yells.

Keisha doesn't look back to see which one said it, but she thinks it sounded like Billy. "Serves him right," she thinks.

Keisha and her brothers need to work on the *Peaceful Conflict Resolution* asset.

Think about your own life. When you have a conflict with someone else, can you work things out in a peaceful way? Are you able to resolve conflicts without using harsh words or violent actions?

If **YES**, keep reading to learn ways to make this asset even stronger.

If **NO**, keep reading to learn ways to add this asset to your life.

> ## Facts!
>
> **Kids with the *Peaceful Conflict Resolution* asset:**
>
> ✔ feel better about school
>
> ✔ feel better about themselves
>
> ✔ are less *aggressive* (pushy and violent)

You can also use these ideas to help add this asset for other people—like your friends, family members, neighbors, and kids at school.

ways to Add This Asset

 **AT HOME**

Use I-Messages. Most conflicts sound a lot like this: "YOU always have to have everything YOUR way!

YOU'RE so stupid! It's all YOUR fault!" People shout, doors slam, no one's happy, and nothing gets solved. With I-messages, you can share your feelings, needs, and point of view without blaming someone else. The basic I-message sounds like this: "I feel ____ when you ____. I need ____." ***Example:*** You're mad at your big sister because she always hogs the phone. Instead of yelling "YOU always hog the phone!" try using an I-message. First, calm yourself down. (See pages 25–26 for how to do this.) Second, say something like this: "I feel frustrated when you stay on the phone for an hour. I need to talk to my friends, too." Then make a suggestion that might solve the conflict: "Can we take equal turns? Like, you get the phone for 20 minutes, and then I get the phone for 20 minutes? We can use the kitchen timer to keep track of the time."

Take Time Outs. You can't control what the other person says or does during a conflict, but you *can* control what *you* say and do. It's not easy—some conflicts stir up your emotions until all you want to do is hurt someone. Back off and take a breather. You might say something like, "Wait—I need a break. Can we talk about this later?" or "Let's stop for a moment and take a time out." Walk away if you can and find a place to calm yourself down and think. Go to your room or another part of your home, write in your journal, listen to some soothing music, and figure out what you want to do next.

Be Willing to Compromise. Some conflicts go on and on because people aren't willing to budge. They don't really care about resolving the conflict. They just want to win. When you compromise, you find a middle ground where *everyone* wins *something*. Start by letting each person describe his or her side. *Example:* You tell your sister, "I need to talk to my friends, too." She says, "Do you have to talk to them at the exact same time I'm on the phone? You have more chances to use the phone than I do. I have softball practice and a lot more homework." How can you both get some of what you want? Maybe you could set up a phone schedule for when you're both home. Or agree to limit your calls to a certain number of minutes. Or use email or instant messaging instead of talking on the phone so much. Give a little, get a little. That's how compromise works.

Have a Family Meeting. Many families meet regularly to talk about plans, problems, and decisions. Family meetings can also be a good way to resolve conflicts peacefully. If you have an ongoing conflict with a sibling, for example, and all your efforts to make peace have failed, then a family meeting might help. Having a parent or another adult present might make it easier for you to share your feelings or resolve the issue once and for all.

Tips for Peaceful Conflict Resolution

★ Describe the problem without blaming the other person. Use I-messages to say what you want and need.

★ Let the other person give his or her point of view. Listen without interrupting. Try to understand where the person is coming from. Put yourself in his or her shoes.

★ Be respectful toward the other person, even when you don't agree.

★ If you get upset, calm yourself. Take a time out if you need to. Agree to meet later to talk more.

★ Come up with ways to resolve your conflict peacefully. Brainstorm as many as you can. Agree to try one for a while, and check in to see how it's working. Be willing to compromise. Try another way if you need to.

★ If the two of you can't resolve your conflict no matter how hard you try, don't give up. Ask a grown-up to listen to both sides and help you find a middle ground. Or you might just agree to disagree. Sometimes that's the best you can do.

 **AT SCHOOL**

Be a Peer Mediator. Does your school have a peer mediation program? Many schools do. Students are trained to help other students resolve conflicts peacefully. It's a great way to learn conflict resolution skills—and to earn respect. If your school has a peer mediation program, see if you can join. If it doesn't, talk with a teacher about starting one.

> **TIP:** Good peer mediators have these qualities: They stay calm. They listen carefully. They avoid taking sides. They're patient. And they really want to help others.

Learn About Famous Peacemakers. Maybe you can do a report on this topic for a school assignment. Pick one or more of these people to study: Nelson Mandela, Mother Teresa, the 14th Dalai Lama, Mahatma Gandhi, Martin Luther King Jr., Ruby Bridges, Bishop Desmond Tutu, President Jimmy Carter. Or choose another peacemaker you want to know more about. Ask your teacher or the media specialist at your school to help you find books, articles, and other types of information about the person.

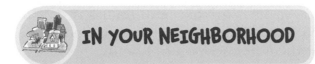

IN YOUR NEIGHBORHOOD

Be a Peacemaker. Stay cool and set a good example. Without putting yourself in danger, try to keep conflicts from turning into fights. This could be as simple as saying, "Hey, guys, let's chill," when friends start arguing. *Caution:* Never get in the middle of a physical fight. Find a grown-up to help.

Use the Power of Politeness. Sometimes saying "Please," "Thanks," "Excuse me," or "No problem" can keep a conflict from starting or turning violent. Okay, so you and a neighbor crashed your bicycles, and it really *was* his fault. But if no one is hurt, why not say, "Sorry, dude!" and laugh it off?

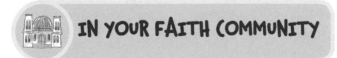

IN YOUR FAITH COMMUNITY

★ Some of history's greatest peacemakers have come out of faith traditions. Dr. Martin Luther King Jr. was a Baptist minister. The 14th Dalai Lama is the leader of the Tibetan Buddhists. Desmond Tutu was an archbishop in the Anglican church. Who are the peacemakers in your faith tradition? Learn more about them. Maybe your religious leader can talk about them in a sermon or homily.

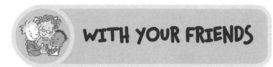

WITH YOUR FRIENDS

★ You offended a friend. Your friend got angry and said something mean about you. Now you're mad, too, and you want to get back at your friend . . . . Wait! Want to put an end to this conflict right now? Apologize! Whether you meant to offend your friend or not, that's what happened. So say you're sorry and mean it. Then you can both move on. What if your friend stays angry and won't forgive you? Give it time. What if you think your friend owes *you* an apology? Get over it—or wait until tempers have cooled, then use an I-message to say how you feel and what you need.

★ If you notice that two of your friends aren't getting along, you might offer to mediate. Listen as each person describes the problem and gives his or her point of view. Ask each person for ideas that might help solve the problem. Don't take sides.

Start Adding!

Pick at least ONE idea you've read here and give it a try. Then think about or write about what happened. Will you try another way to be a more peaceful person and resolve conflicts without violence?

Back to Keisha's Story

"Dad!" Keisha yells. "Dad! Billy and Jerome are fighting! Dad, where are you?!"

Keisha's dad appears at the door with a serious look on his face. He's holding the telephone against his chest. He says, "Shhh . . . Keisha, this is an important call. Why are you yelling, anyway?" His voice is calm and even.

Keisha takes a deep breath and tries to be calm, like her dad is. "It's the boys. They're wrestling and hogging the ball."

Her dad nods and looks out the doorway. Keisha turns around and sees that her brothers have stood up but are still arguing.

"Do you remember that talk we all had about a week ago—the one about solving problems peacefully?" her dad asks.

Keisha remembers. Suddenly, she knows what to do. She kisses her dad on the cheek and goes back to her brothers.

As she approaches, they look at her with scowls on their faces. "What?" demands Billy.

Keisha makes a point of not raising her voice. "You guys are the best at helping me with my kicks. And I really like it that you let me hang out with you. But when you start pounding on each other, I feel like it's no fun being around you."

They stand there staring at her. Keisha waits but doesn't say another word.

Then Jerome cracks a smile. "You look pretty fierce, Keisha. Like Mom when we tease her about her cooking."

"Watch out," Billy adds. "This girl can really kick some sense into people." He jokingly rubs his leg and says, "Ooh, that still hurts—you've got some power in that right foot, you know?"

Keisha smiles and says, "Sorry about that. I was mad earlier, but I shouldn't have actually *kicked* you."

"Yeah," Jerome adds. "Save it for the ball, will ya?"

Keisha asks, "So . . . we're good? No more fighting?"

Her brothers smile, shake hands, and pass the football back to her. Keisha feels proud of them—and of herself, too.

A NOTE TO GROWN-UPS

Ongoing research by Search Institute, a nonprofit organization based in Minneapolis, Minnesota, shows that young people who succeed have specific assets in their lives—**Developmental Assets** including family support, a caring neighborhood, integrity, resistance skills, self-esteem, and a sense of purpose. This book, along with the other seven books in the **Adding Assets Series for Kids**, empowers young people ages 8–12 to build their own Developmental Assets.

But it's very important to acknowledge that building assets for and with young people is primarily an *adult* responsibility. What kids need most in their lives are grown-ups—parents and other relatives, teachers, school administrators, neighbors, youth leaders, religious leaders, community members, policy makers, advocates, and more—who care about them as individuals. They need adults who care enough to learn their names, to show interest in their lives, to listen when they talk, to provide them with opportunities to realize their potential, to teach them well, to give them sound advice, to serve as good examples, to guide them, to inspire them, to support them when they stumble, and to shield them from harm—as much as is humanly possible these days.

This book focuses on five of the 40 Developmental Assets identified by Search Institute. These are **Internal Assets**—values, skills, and self-perceptions that kids develop *internally,* with your help. The internal assets described here are called the **Social Competencies Assets.** They're about forming the skills and attitudes kids need to make it in the world.

Psychologist and author John Rosemond wrote, "Stop thinking that your first obligation is to keep your children happy. It isn't. Your first obligation is to endow them with the skills they'll need to pursue happiness on their own." These are the social competencies: knowing how to plan ahead and make decisions, deal with new and challenging situations, form satisfying relationships with others (including those from different racial, ethnic, and cultural backgrounds—our world is rapidly becoming more diverse), stay out of trouble, and resolve conflicts peacefully. Children with these skills are well-equipped to cope with the choices and challenges they meet in life and develop into healthy, competent adults.

A list of all 40 Developmental Assets for middle childhood, with definitions, follows. If you want to know more about the assets, some of the resources listed on pages 84–85 will help you. Or you can visit the Search Institute Web site at *www.search-institute.org.*

Thank you for caring enough about kids to make this book available to the young person or persons in your life. We'd love to hear your success stories, and we welcome your suggestions for adding assets to kids' lives—or improving future editions of this book.

Pamela Espeland and Elizabeth Verdick
Free Spirit Publishing Inc.
217 Fifth Avenue North, Suite 200
Minneapolis, MN 55401-1299
help4kids@freespirit.com

The 40 Developmental Assets for Middle Childhood

EXTERNAL ASSETS

SUPPORT

1. **Family support**—Family life provides high levels of love and support.
2. **Positive family communication**—Parent(s) and child communicate positively. Child feels comfortable seeking advice and counsel from parent(s).
3. **Other adult relationships**—Child receives support from adults other than her or his parent(s).
4. **Caring neighborhood**—Child experiences caring neighbors.
5. **Caring school climate**—Relationships with teachers and peers provide a caring, encouraging school environment.
6. **Parent involvement in schooling**—Parent(s) are actively involved in helping the child succeed in school.

EMPOWERMENT

7. **Community values children**—Child feels valued and appreciated by adults in the community.
8. **Children as resources**—Child is included in decisions at home and in the community.
9. **Service to others**—Child has opportunities to help others in the community.
10. **Safety**—Child feels safe at home, at school, and in her or his neighborhood.

BOUNDARIES AND EXPECTATIONS

11. **Family boundaries**—Family has clear and consistent rules and consequences and monitors the child's whereabouts.
12. **School boundaries**—School provides clear rules and consequences.
13. **Neighborhood boundaries**—Neighbors take responsibility for monitoring the child's behavior.
14. **Adult role models**—Parent(s) and other adults in the child's family, as well as nonfamily adults, model positive, responsible behavior.
15. **Positive peer influence**—Child's closest friends model positive, responsible behavior.
16. **High expectations**—Parent(s) and teachers expect the child to do her or his best at school and in other activities.

CONSTRUCTIVE USE OF TIME

17. **Creative activities**—Child participates in music, art, drama, or creative writing two or more times per week.
18. **Child programs**—Child participates two or more times per week in cocurricular school activities or structured community programs for children.
19. **Religious community**—Child attends religious programs or services one or more times per week.
20. **Time at home**—Child spends some time most days both in high-quality interaction with parent(s) and doing things at home other than watching TV or playing video games.

The 40 Developmental Assets list may be reproduced for educational, noncommercial uses only.
Copyright © 2004 by Search Institute, 800-888-7828; *www.search-institute.org.*

INTERNAL ASSETS

COMMITMENT TO LEARNING

21. **Achievement motivation**—Child is motivated and strives to do well in school.
22. **Learning engagement**—Child is responsive, attentive, and actively engaged in learning at school and enjoys participating in learning activities outside of school.
23. **Homework**—Child usually hands in homework on time.
24. **Bonding to adults at school**—Child cares about teachers and other adults at school.
25. **Reading for pleasure**—Child enjoys and engages in reading for fun most days of the week.

POSITIVE VALUES

26. **Caring**—Parent(s) tell the child it is important to help other people.
27. **Equality and social justice**—Parent(s) tell the child it is important to speak up for equal rights for all people.
28. **Integrity**—Parent(s) tell the child it is important to stand up for one's beliefs.
29. **Honesty**—Parent(s) tell the child it is important to tell the truth.
30. **Responsibility**—Parent(s) tell the child it is important to accept personal responsibility for behavior.
31. **Healthy lifestyle**—Parent(s) tell the child it is important to have good health habits and an understanding of healthy sexuality.

SOCIAL COMPETENCIES

32. **Planning and decision making**—Child thinks about decisions and is usually happy with the results of her or his decisions.
33. **Interpersonal competence**—Child cares about and is affected by other people's feelings, enjoys making friends, and, when frustrated or angry, tries to calm herself or himself.
34. **Cultural competence**—Child knows and is comfortable with people of different racial, ethnic, and cultural backgrounds and with her or his own cultural identity.
35. **Resistance skills**—Child can stay away from people who are likely to get her or him in trouble and is able to say no to doing wrong or dangerous things.
36. **Peaceful conflict resolution**—Child attempts to resolve conflict nonviolently.

POSITIVE IDENTITY

37. **Personal power**—Child feels he or she has some influence over things that happen in her or his life.
38. **Self-esteem**—Child likes and is proud to be the person he or she is.
39. **Sense of purpose**—Child sometimes thinks about what life means and whether there is a purpose for her or his life.
40. **Positive view of personal future**—Child is optimistic about her or his personal future.

The 40 Developmental Assets list may be reproduced for educational, noncommercial uses only.
Copyright © 2004 by Search Institute, 800-888-7828; *www.search-institute.org*.

Helpful Resources

Books

Get Organized Without Losing It by Janet S. Fox (Minneapolis: Free Spirit Publishing, 2006). Learn to manage your tasks, your time, and major messes (like your backpack, desk, and locker) with this helpful, humorous guide. You'll have less stress and more fun.

The Kids' Guide to Working Out Conflicts: How to Keep Cool, Stay Safe, and Get Along by Naomi Drew (Minneapolis: Free Spirit Publishing, 2004). Being teased? Feeling threatened? Can't agree? This book gives you the knowledge and skills to avoid conflict, defuse tough situations, stand up for yourself, and more.

Reaching Your Goals by Robin Landew Silverman (New York: Franklin Watts, 2004). To turn a wish into a goal takes creative thinking and organized planning skills. This book shows how to make a plan and see it through to the end.

Speak Up and Get Along! by Scott Cooper (Minneapolis: Free Spirit Publishing, 2005). This book is a handy toolbox of 21 ways to express yourself, build relationships, end arguments and fights, halt bullying, beat unhappy feelings, and more.

Think for Yourself: A Kid's Guide to Solving Life's Dilemmas and Other Sticky Problems by Cynthia MacGregor (Toronto: Lobster Press, 2003). This book breaks down daily problems into categories: friends, family, grown-ups, and everyday situations. Real-life examples and choices for solutions help you learn to think things through and make good decisions.

Web sites

Students Against Violence Everywhere (SAVE)
www.nationalsave.org
Learn about alternatives to violence. Practice what you learn in school and community service projects. This national organization was started by a student and a teacher and is run by a student board.

Youth Service America
www.servenet.org
Connect to organizations and service projects in your area. Type in your ZIP code, skills, and interests to find the best experience for you.

Youth Venture
www.youthventure.org
Youth Venture believes every young person can make a difference. Do you have a solution to a problem in your community? Youth Venture invests in the ideas of young people who create, launch, and lead organizations, clubs, or businesses that provide a positive, lasting benefit in a school, neighborhood, or large community.

Books

Building Assets Is Elementary: Group Activities for Helping Kids Ages 8–12 Succeed by Search Institute (Minneapolis: Search Institute, 2004). Promoting creativity, time-management skills, kindness, manners, and more, this flexible activity book includes over 50 easy-to-use group exercises for the classroom or youth group.

Character Building Day by Day by Anne D. Mather and Louise B. Weldon (Minneapolis: Free Spirit Publishing, 2006). Brief, engaging stories help children grow up to be successful, contributing adults. An excellent tool for classrooms, youth groups, and character-conscious homes.

The Life-Smart Kid: Teaching Your Child to Use Good Judgment in Every Situation by Lawrence J. Greene (Rocklin, CA: Prima Publication, 1995). Discover practical ways to help young people develop critical thinking and decision-making skills.

The Unwritten Rules of Friendship: Simple Strategies to Help Your Child Make Friends by Natalie Madorsky Elman, Ph.D., and Eileen Kennedy-Moore, Ph.D. (New York: Little, Brown, 2003). This book describes how certain behaviors can cause difficulties when interacting with peers. A great resource educators and parents can use to improve children's social skills.

What Kids Need to Succeed: Proven, Practical Ways to Raise Good Kids by Peter L. Benson, Ph.D., Judy Galbraith, M.A., and Pamela Espeland (Minneapolis: Free Spirit Publishing, 1994). More than 900 specific, concrete suggestions help adults help children build Developmental Assets at home, at school, and in the community.

Web sites

Alliance for Youth
www.americaspromise.org
Founded after the Presidents' Summit for America's Future in 1997, this organization is committed to fulfilling five promises to American youth: Every child needs caring adults, safe places, a healthy start, marketable skills, and opportunities to serve. This collaborative network includes resources, information, and opportunities for involvement.

Learning Peace
www.learningpeace.com
This site for teachers, parents, and administrators will help you create more peace in your schools, homes, and communities. By teaching and modeling conflict resolution, anger management, anti-bullying, and character building, you can create more peaceful interactions among the kids you know.

National Mentoring Partnership
www.mentoring.org
A wealth of information about becoming and finding a mentor, this organization provides connections, training, resources, and advice to introduce and support mentoring partnerships.

Search Institute
www.search-institute.org
Through dynamic research and analysis, this independent nonprofit organization works to promote healthy, active, and content youth and communities.

Index

About the Authors

Both Pamela Espeland and Elizabeth Verdick have written many books for children and teens.

Pamela is the coauthor (with Peter L. Benson and Judy Galbraith) of *What Kids Need to Succeed* and *What Teens Need to Succeed* and the author of *Succeed Every Day*, all based on Search Institute's concept of the 40 Developmental Assets. She is the author of *Life Lists for Teens* and the coauthor (with Gershen Kaufman and Lev Raphael) of *Stick Up for Yourself!*

Elizabeth is a children's book writer and editor. She is the author of *Germs Are Not for Sharing, Tails Are Not for Pulling, Teeth Are Not for Biting, Words Are Not for Hurting,* and *Feet Are Not for Kicking,* and coauthor (with Marjorie Lisovskis) of *How to Take the GRRRR Out of Anger* and (with Trevor Romain) of *Stress Can Really Get on Your Nerves!* and *True or False? Tests Stink!*

Pamela and Elizabeth first worked together on *Making Every Day Count* and have since teamed up to write *Dude, That's Rude!* and *See You Later, Procrastinator!* They live in Minnesota with their families and pets.

More Titles in the Adding Assets Series for Kids

Each book is 80–100 pages, softcover, two-color, illustrated, 5⅛" x 7". For ages 8–12.

People Who Care About You

Kids build the six Support Assets: Family Support, Positive Family Communication, Other Adult Relationships, Caring Neighborhood, Caring School Climate, and Parent Involvement in Schooling.

Doing and Being Your Best

Kids build the six Boundaries and Expectations Assets: Family Boundaries, School Boundaries, Neighborhood Boundaries, Adult Role Models, Positive Peer Influence, and High Expectations.

Smart Ways to Spend Your Time

Kids build the four Constructive Use of Time Assets: Creative Activities, Child Programs, Religious Community, and Time at Home.

Loving to Learn

Kids build the five Commitment to Learning Assets: Achievement Motivation, Learning Engagement, Homework, Bonding to Adults at School, and Reading for Pleasure.

Knowing and Doing What's Right

Kids build the six Positive Values Assets: Caring, Equality and Social Justice, Integrity, Honesty, Responsibility, and Healthy Lifestyle.

Helping Out and Staying Safe

Kids build the four Empowerment Assets: Community Values Children, Children as Resources, Service to Others, and Safety.

Proud to Be You

Kids build the four Positive Identity Assets: Personal Power, Self-Esteem, Sense of Purpose, and Positive View of Personal Future.

A Leader's Guide to The Adding Assets Series for Kids

A comprehensive, easy-to-use curriculum for building all 40 Developmental Assets, with activities, discussion prompts, handouts for parents and other family adults, and a scope-and-sequence for standards-based education. The included CD-ROM features all of the reproducible forms from the book and an additional 40 pages of student handouts used in the sessions. For grades 3–6.

288 pp.; softcover; lay-flat binding; 8½" x 11".

For pricing information, to place an order, or to request a free catalog, contact:

Free Spirit Publishing Inc.
217 Fifth Avenue North • Suite 200 • Minneapolis, MN 55401-1299
toll-free 800.735.7323 • local 612.338.2068 • fax 612.337.5050
help4kids@freespirit.com • www.freespirit.com